KEYBOARDING
for the electronic office

Audio assisted self-instruction or class course

Edith Mackay

PITMAN PUBLISHING
128 Long Acre, London, WC2E 9AN

A Division of Longman Group UK Limited

© Edith Mackay 1986

First published in Great Britain 1986
Reprinted 1988, 1989

British Library Cataloguing in Publication Data
Mackay, Edith
  Keyboarding for the electronic office: audio-assisted
  self-instruction or class course.
  1. Electronic data processing—keyboarding
  I. Title
  001.64'42   QA76.9.K48

Text photoset by Tek-Art, Croydon, Surrey
Printed and bound in Singapore

ISBN 0 273 02353 5

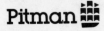

Contents

Introduction

With electronic QWERTY keyboards now so widely established in business, professional, educational, and home use, keyboarding is a lifelong asset to anyone. 'Touch' keyboarding is an easily-acquired skill — provided expert guidance and practice material are followed.

Keyboarding for the electronic age is a student-centred, self-pacing course, which is equally suitable for self-instruction or class use.

The companion **cassette** will greatly assist the self-learner to master new reaches in a controlled rhythmic manner, with orderly coordination of eye, mind, and fingers. It also gives valuable technical advice. In a class situation, the cassette will enable the teacher to concentrate his/her attention on observing and correcting student performance. The use of individual cassette players and earphones enables each student to progress at his/her optimum rate, unhindered by extraneous noise.

Aims of this course

Those who complete the course will be able to:

1 Use a keyboard to input alphabetic/numeric/symbol text at a *minimum* speed of 4500 key depressions per hour (75 kdpm) with 99% accuracy. (This is the basic requirement of the Royal Society of Arts **Keyboard Skills** examination.) Most learners, however, will achieve a considerably higher speed than this with 99% accuracy.
2 Use a numeric keypad for all-figure data with similar speed and accuracy.
3 Understand basic concepts and terminology used in information processing by keyboard operations.
4 Proceed efficiently to master extensions of keyboarding skill — such as typing, word processing, and computing.

Nothing is learned which later needs unlearning. *A solid foundation is provided on which to build a variety of career structures.*

Approach of the course

The sustained cumulative approach ensures that there is *constant reinforcement of learning*: no key is allowed to get rusty. In line with today's keyboarding needs, due attention is given to figures/symbols mastery.

Essential accuracy/speed development on continuous text begins in the third unit and is included in every subsequent unit: likewise with alphanumeric strings. The learner measures his/her progress from page to page, recording results in the boxes provided for comparative self-appraisal. (Only key depression rates with at least 99% accuracy are recorded.) Class teachers not wishing learners to write in the text books should devise a suitable Record Form (see page 2).

The logical and skill-building pattern of this course will promote confidence and rapid progress.

Duration of course

Each unit can be completed in *approximately 30 minutes*, depending on individual aptitude and the number of times each line is repeated.

Thus the whole course of 32 units can be completed in approximately 16 hours (in line with the RSA's recommended course time of approximately 15 hours for beginners — see page 52).

In a school or college, **Keyboarding for the Electronic Office** can be comfortably timetabled within a single term — a good investment of such little time to acquire a lifelong valuable skill.

Acknowledgements

Thanks go to the Royal Society of Arts Examinations Board for giving permission to reproduce two of their past **Keyboarding Skills** examination papers: thanks also to the Pitman Examinations Institute for permission to reproduce a past **Keyboarding** examination paper. The author also expresses warm thanks to Denise Harris of Pitman for her meticulous and helpful work on the text.

Record forms

Suggested layout for A4 Record Forms to monitor kpdm.

(Units 3-14)   **(Units 15-32)**   **(Units 15-21)**

1 minute		*1 minute* *paragraphs*	*2 minutes*		*3 minutes*	
sentences	*strings*		*sentences*	*strings*	*sentences*	*strings*

(Units 22-25)   **(Units 22-32)**   **(Units 26-32)**

5 minutes *sentences*	*7 minutes* *sentences*	*3 minutes* *strings*	*4 minutes* *strings*	*8 minutes* *sentences*	*10 minutes* *sentences*

Keyboarding for the Electronic Office cassette (ISBN 0 273 02555 4)

The cassette to accompany this book is available from: Pitman Publishing Limited, 128 Long Acre, London WC2E 9AN. Price is £3.99 including VAT.

Cheques and postal orders (UK) or Bankers Drafts (overseas) should be made payable to 'Pitman Publishing Limited'. Bank notes should be sent by registered post. We accept payment by Barclaycard, Access, American Express and Diners Club.

Machines using QWERTY keyboards

(In all cases there are differences from make to make
and from model to model.)

1 Manual typewriters

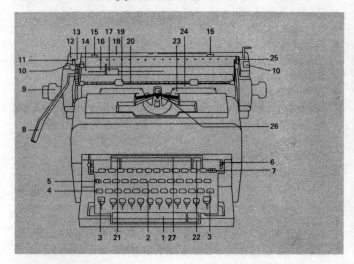

2 Electric typewriters

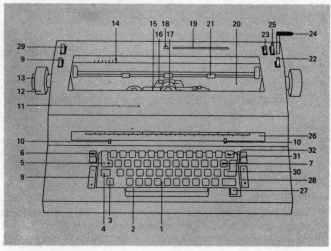

1 Manual typewriters

1 Space bar
2 Keyboard
3 Shift keys
4 Shift lock
5 Margin release key
6 Ribbon/stencil switch
7 Backspace key
8 Carriage return lever
9 Cylinder knobs
10 Carriage release
controls
11 Interliner
12 Carriage
13 Line space regulator
14 Paper table
15 Margin stops
16 Paper edge guide scale
17 Paper edge guide
18 Margin scale
19 Paper bail and rollers
20 Paper bail scale
21 Tab set key
22 Tab clear key
23 Alignment scales
24 Cylinder
25 Paper release lever
26 Printing point
27 Tab bar

2 Electric typewriters

1 Keyboard
2 Space bar
3 Shift keys
4 Shift lock
5 Tab key
6 Margin release key
7 Express backspace key
8 Tab set/clear control
9 Half spacing selector
10 Margin stops
11 Ribbon/stencil switch
12 Cylinder knobs
13 Variable line spacer
14 Paper edge guide
15 Ribbon carrier
16 Alignment scales
17 Type element (golf
ball)
18 Paper support release
19 Paper support
20 Cylinder
21 Paper bail and rollers
22 Interliner
23 Line space regulator
24 Paper injector/ejector
25 Paper release lever
26 Front scale
27 Correction key
28 On/off switch
29 Pitch selector
30 Type element return
key
31 Index key
32 Backspace key

3 Electronic typewriters

Microprocessor controlled, these have revolutionized typewriter operation. The following (alphabetical) list gives features not found on manual and electric machines.

- Automatic carrier return, centring, underlining, right-alignment (eg for date in letters), right-margin justification, and indexing (movement of paper up or down by depression of a key).
- Backspacing versatility, with express backtracking, or one character at a time, or in increments of 1/60 of an inch.
- Bold typing facility for emphasis.
- Corrections are simple. A window display panel enables the typist to detect and correct errors in the text *before* it is committed to paper or memory.
- Memory will automatically print out date, signature block, short texts, etc, as well as reproduce page formats. Where machines have a sufficiently large memory it is possible to mail merge, eg a list of names and addresses within a circular letter.
- Operator prompts, eg to show the remaining amount of memory, or when an instruction to the machine is not given properly.
- Paper is automatically fed into the machine by pressing the paper-set key. The typing position from the top of the page is programmable.
- Paper-end indicator (also programmable).
- Repeat typing for all keys.
- Ribbon changes are quick and clean with the cassette system.
- Ruling facility for horizontal and vertical lines.
- Scientific, mathematical, and foreign language text is undertaken by use of the appropriate daisy wheel or (with IBM machines) golf ball print element.
- Search operation. In edit mode a letter, symbol, word or line can be set for search.
- Second keyboard for seldom-used symbols, brought into operation by moving a switch, eg to KB II.
- Tabulation is simplified by automatic column layout. For fast statistical typing the automatic decimal tabulator correctly aligns columns of decimal figures.
- Typeface and pitch changeover is simple by use of different daisy wheels.

Keyboard arrangement of the Silver Reed Ex 66 electronic typewriter

4 Word processors

These electronic machines are designed to work primarily with text (words, figures, etc, in paragraphs and columns in documents): thus they are also known as text editors.

As text is keyed in at the keyboard, it appears on a TV-like screen and is electronically filed. If the text then requires text-editing (insertions, deletions, paragraph rearrangement, etc) *only the changes or instructions are keyed in*. Correct text is untouched. After text-editing the material automatically adjusts back into lines of the set length. Only after the text is finalized is it printed on paper — as many copies as are required.

Electronic typewriters have many features in common with word processors. The 2 most important differences between them are:

a   Far greater storage capability of word processors.
b   Word processors have a TV-like screen as distinct from an electronic typewriter's thin window display panel.

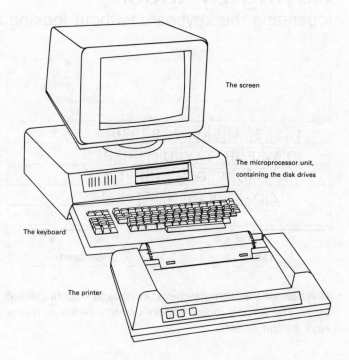

The screen

The microprocessor unit, containing the disk drives

The keyboard

The printer

5 Computers

A computer is an electronic system, capable of storing and processing large amounts of information. It roughly resembles a word processor in appearance, each computer or computer terminal having a keyboard and a TV-like screen.

Whereas a word processor is chiefly concerned with text and communications, a computer is a general-purpose machine with sophisticated information processing capabilities. Computer programs (devised by computer programmers) are used in the processing of information: these are sets of machine instructions in a computer language (BASIC, COBOL, FORTRAN, etc) which are automatically carried out by the system in sequence. Often inputting is by keyboard, and outputting by printer.

Microcomputers are widely used in the home and in education.

Additional information on electronic systems is given in the accuracy/speed paragraphs on pages 43 – 48.

Keying by touch
(operating the keyboard without looking at it)

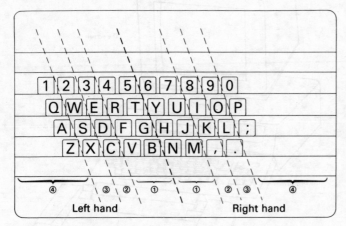

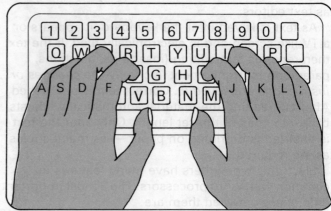

Division of the alphanumeric keyboard into fingering units. The strong index fingers operate twice as many keys as the others.

Fingers over the home keys — the base from which all other keys are located.

Each of the eight fingers controls its own keys, as shown, moving upwards, downwards or across from the central position over the home keys (asdf/jkl;).
In this way the operator acquires the skill of striking the correct keys without looking at the keyboard: the eyes are free to read the copy.

The location of the alphabet and figure keys is similar on different types and make of machine.

Therefore **once mastered, keyboard skill is easily adapted to any other QWERTY keyboard**.

The position of symbols, fractions, etc, can vary from machine to machine. Therefore remove the keyboard chart at the back of this book, and complete it by neatly writing in these characters as they appear on *your* keyboard. You will need to refer to this when you have completed the alphabet and figure units.

Preparing to key

A comfortable **sitting position** is important for lengthy spells at the keyboard to prevent aches and tiredness (and thereby increase productivity).

Use a purpose-designed upholstered **chair** with a back support: adjust the seat height and your distance from the keyboard for relaxed comfort, neither stretching nor crouching. Feet should be flat on the floor for balance.

Prop up the **book** so that it is sloping towards you, to avoid eye strain. (If you are using — or likely to use — a manual typewriter, place the copy *to your right* — to prevent your hand sweeping between eyes and copy each time the carriage is returned.)
Lighting should be good enough for reading the copy without strain — artificial lights situated above you, or behind you (on the same side as the copy). If you are using a word processor or computer, the lighting intensity and angle of the screen should be adjusted for comfort.

The **position of the hands** is important for expert keying. Fingers should be curved, and just clearing the home keys, thumbs over the space bar. Do *not* rest your wrists on the framework of the machine. Strike the space bar with the side of the thumb as shown.

Key striking

Electric and electronic keyboards need only slight pressure with the tips of the fingers to activate them and produce good even impressions.
Manual typewriters — each key needs to be struck firmly and sharply for good even impressions.

Starting new lines

On word processors, computers, and most electronic typewriters (in automatic mode) new lines are started automatically once margins are set. It is also possible to return the carrier by pressing the RETURN key.

Electric and electronic typewriters (the latter in normal typewriter mode). The return of the carriage (in the case of type-bar machines) or the printhead (with single-element machines with a daisy wheel or golf ball head) is automatic when the RETURN key is operated by the right-hand little finger.

Manual typewriters — at the end of lines, operate the carriage return lever with a quick sweep of the left hand and forearm. The hand should be held flat, with the palm down and fingers closed, and should strike the lever with just enough force to ensure that the carriage reaches the left margin stop.

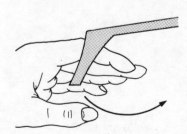

Know your machine

Since different kinds of machine will be used for keying from this text (manual, electric and electronic typewriters; word processors; computers) detailed machine operating instructions cannot be given.

Learners should consult their operating manual (or, better still, an experienced operator) to determine the basics of operation. Therefore, before you begin, *become familiar with your machine*. Scrutinise it alongside its manual, noting the location of the main parts and controls, and how they work.

For example, typewriter operators need to know how to:

- insert, straighten, and remove paper
- set margins — for a 40 line-length on A4 paper (approx 8¼ x 11¾") the left margin position will be at:

  21 for 10-pitch (10 characters to one inch or 25 mm)

  30 for 12-pitch (12 characters to one inch or 25 mm)

  42 for 15-pitch (15 characters to one inch or 25 mm)

- select line-spacing required
- start a new line

Keying the units

The given line-length of 40 characters should be used. Keyed matter will look best with equal margins right and left (for typewriter settings see above).

At least one inch of blank space should be left at the top and bottom of paper. Use single line-spacing when repeating a line, but leave a line of space (by turning up twice) before proceeding to a different line: this will ease checking.

Key each line *at least twice*, preferably until you can key it fluently, speedily, and accurately — without looking at the keyboard and using the correct finger for each key.

Screen-based operators should obtain a print-out of their copy. It will be difficult to monitor accuracy/speed development satisfactorily without this hard copy.

Unit 1 Alphabet

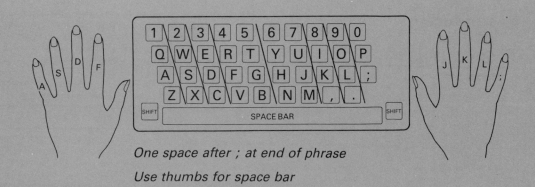

One space after ; at end of phrase

Use thumbs for space bar

Technique tips

Keep all fingers over the home keys.
Say each letter (and space) to yourself as you key it, and 'think' the finger you use.

Instructions

Copy each line (40 line-length) exactly as shown until you can key it accurately and fluently. *Do not attempt to correct any errors you make.* From time to time ring your errors. If a particular key causes problems, pay it special attention when repeating the lines.

Note ⊡ signals cassette tape on, ⊙ cassette tape off.

Home key drills

⊡aaa sss ddd fff jjj kkk lll ;;; asdfjkl;

asdf jkl; asdf jkl; asdf jkl; asdf jkl;;

Home key words

a as ass lass alas all fall falls flasks

a ad add adds lads ask asks jaffa jaffas⊙

a as dad dads fads lad lads salad salads

Home key phrases

a sad lad; a sad dad; sad lass; all sad;

flasks fall; lads fall; dads fall; alas;

a jaffa salad; alaska salad; all salads;

add a jaffa; add jaffa salad; ask a lad;

Unit 2 Alphabet

Introducing

Feet firmly on floor

*Eyes on copy **not** on keyboard*

At the start of a lesson always use one or 2 lines from the bottom of the previous page as warm-up practice.
Review the important technique tips and instructions given in Unit 1.

Always 'feel' a new reach before starting to key:

1 All fingers over the home keys
2 Look at keyboard and move finger to new key and back
3 Practice the same movement *without* looking at the keyboard
4 Proceed to keying the location drill

G location drill

● ffg ffg ffg fgg fgg fgg fgf fgf fgf fggf

G words using all known letters

fag fags gaff gaffs gad gads saga sagas; ○

jag jags flag flags jag jags gala galas;

ask slag glad glass lag lags gall galls;

H location drill

● jjh jjh jjh jhh jhh jhh jhj jhj jhj jhhj ○

H words using all known letters

has had hall halls sash lash flash slash ○

ash hag hags shall half shah shahs allah

jah has haka halls dash gash slash flash

Develop accuracy/ fluency on all known letters

a lass has had a jaffa salad; ask a hag;

slash all flash flags as sad shahs fall;

dad has had half a flask; jag all flags;

glass flasks shall fall as hags jag lags

10

Unit 3 Alphabet

Introducing

E   O

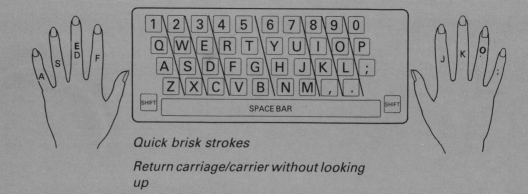

Quick brisk strokes

Return carriage/carrier without looking up

Continue to copy each line exactly as shown until you can key it accurately and fluently. Do not correct any errors you make.

Testing and recording accuracy/ speed

Spend the last few minutes of each practice period as follows:

a   Time yourself for exactly one minute on the lines above the numbered bar, correcting any errors by the quickest effective method on your machine

b   Count your key depressions (with the aid of the numbered bar) up to your first uncorrected error, if there is one, and write this figure in the first marginal box. Add one to your total each time you started a new line (for carriage/carrier returns)

Then repeat a and b above on the two lines of letter strings below the bar.

E   **location drill**

●dde dde dde dee dee dee ded ded ded deed

E   **words using all known letters**

deed seed heed dead deal fade jade shade ◻

ease less keel feel heel deaf leaf sheaf

eggs legs kegs eels sake fake lake shake

O   **location drill**

●llo llo llo loo loo loo lol lol lol lool

O   **words using all known letters**

do does of off dog jog fog log look hook ◻

go goes oh hod god sod odd old sold gold

so solo ho hog ode doe oak ego soak doll

Develop then test accuracy/speed on all known letters

she looked so jaded as she jogged ahead;

as she sold gold goods he fed a sad dog;

he feels a fool as he loads glass dolls;

she does good deeds; he sells fake jade;

5	10	15	20	25	30	35	40

. . . . Kdpm

fls a;l jsd hfj gls efl oja keo; jso hak

ego kad jlf els ojk goa osk ;ajo seh oad

. . . . Kdpm

Unit 4 Alphabet

Introducing capitals and

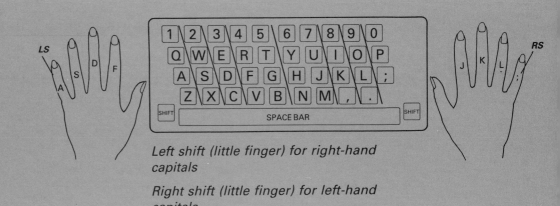

Left shift (little finger) for right-hand capitals

Right shift (little finger) for left-hand capitals

Keying a left-hand capital letter

1 Remove right hand from home keys and hold down right shift key with the little finger
2 Key the required letter with left hand
3 Return right hand to home keys

Right-hand capitals

Follow the same procedure but use opposite hands.

Testing and recording accuracy/ speed

Add one to your key depressions total for each capital letter (for use of shift key).

Left-hand capitals

aA; sS; dD; fF; gG; eE; Ale Sad Dad Fall

⊙ Gala Ease Alas Seed Deed Food Goose Ella ◎

Right-hand capitals

lLa kKa jJa hHa oOa Loss Keg Jade He Ode

⊙ Lad Keel Joe Has Oak Log Koo Jed Had Ode ◎

⸱ full stop

⊙ ll. ll. ll. l.. l.. l.. l.l l.l l.l l..

Ask. Look. See. Jog. Do. Hold. Ah. ◎ *2 spaces after full stop*

Develop then test accuracy/speed on all known keys

Floods shook Kos. Al dead. A sad saga.

Do a good deed. Also look good as gold.

A glass flask falls as flash Jess flees.

Jake sells eggs; Della sells sea shells.

. . . . Kdpm

5	10	15	20	25	30	35	40

fDk Laf Js; dSj oEj fAe Kgs Hal Dos kGl;

Fla Osa fS; Aok Elh Ggj lOk jJa aKl kOl;

. . . . Kdpm

Unit 5 Alphabet

Introducing

R   I

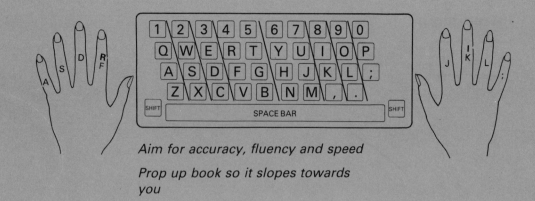

Aim for accuracy, fluency and speed

Prop up book so it slopes towards you

Testing and recording accuracy/ speed

99% accuracy is required (only one uncorrected key depression per hundred). Therefore if your key depressions total *less than 100* (approximately 2½ lines) record in the box your total up to the first uncorrected error.
If your key depressions total *more than 100* (but less than 200) record in the box your total up to the second uncorrected error.

R location drill

● ffr ffr ffr frr frr frr frf frf frf frrf

R words using all known letters

red rod far oar sore lore door fork dark ▣

are for her jar here hear dear deer free

ear era err rag roof rear sear jeer jerk

I location drill

● kki kki kki kii kii kii kik kik kik kiik

I words using all known letters

kid did lid rid risk silk life girl jail ▣

his lie air aid laid raid said like fire

sir fir ail oil fill kill hill ride side

Develop then test accuracy/speed on all known letters

Freddie adores Jillie for her fair hair.
Lisa asked for silk roses for her dress.
Ask Reggie for fried eggs or fried fish.
Sarah had looked hard for her red glass.

.... Kdpm

| 5   10   15   20   25   30   35   40

sAj kLf sG; hKl eDj fRo kId jOs aHo jEl;

jSa kFi sJ; fLk fIk lAj sHo fRl gOk sEo;

.... Kdpm

13

Unit 6   Alphabet

Unit 6 · Alphabet

Introducing

Little fingers for shift keys

One space after ; two after .

Testing and recording accuracy/ speed

If you finish the material before the timing is up, start it again.

| W | **location drill** | ● ssw ssw ssw sww sww sww sws sws sws swws |

W	**words using all known letters**	was wed wig who were well wall will wake ○
		few sew sow how wire wear wore work show
		law saw jaw low flow week wife wide wood

| U | **location drill** | ● jju jju jju juu juu juu juj juj juj juuj |

U	**words using all known letters**	jug jugs dull our ours dues would suffer ○
		hug hugs huge rug rugs duke issue refuse
		use uses used auk sure suds suede figure

Develop then test accuracy/speed on all known letters

I worked a whole week for Will Rosewall.
Lulu Rule was so sure of her good looks.
He asked Widow Woodhall for gold jewels.
Doug was well aware our fare was frugal.

. . . . Kdpm

| | 5 | 10 | 15 | 20 | 25 | 30 | 35 | 40 |

aK Luj ;Der kJ dRkl sGlo Ila jU jSa kHl;
jFo jUk lKad fWl Ejs Ika al;f dIk jGa Kl

. . . . Kdpm

Unit 7 Alphabet

Introducing

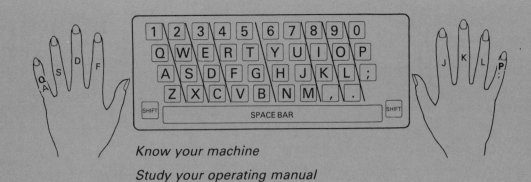

Know your machine

Study your operating manual

Q **location drill**	⦿ aaq aaq aaq aqq aqq aqq aqa aqa aqa aqqa	
Q **words using all known letters**	quads squad Jaques equal equals equalled ⊙ queue quiff square quire liquor squiggle quirk squid squash squaw sequel squeaked	
P **location drill**	⦿ ;;p ;;p ;;p ;pp ;pp ;pp ;p; ;p; ;p; ;pp;	
P **words using all known letters**	pad paid pod pure gap gape hop hope rope ⊙ pea pear peg pegs dip pass fop pale pill pig jeep par park rap wrap lip quip page	

Develop then test accuracy/speed on all known letters

Pippa has prepared all our April orders.
Quaker Square has a row of queer houses.
Please allow equal shares for all of us.
Paula will require a well judged sequel.

.... Kdpm

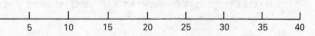

Sl fAk sLk Jfd Hwl;g Juilo Pafu Qulj; Fe
iDef jUlo Ga lP; kIok dFre Rqj dWio; lOd

.... Kdpm

Unit 8 Alphabet

Introducing

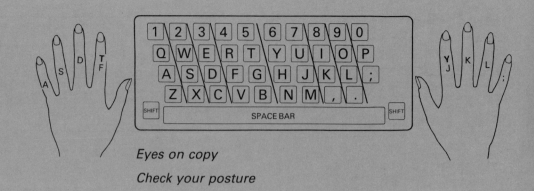

Eyes on copy

Check your posture

T **location drill**

fft fft fft ftt ftt ftt ftf ftf ftf fttf

T **words using all known letters**

at the this these left right fight start

it its that those deft state quite quote

to too just stake stow their there plate

Y **location drill**

jjy jjy jjy jyy jyy jyy jyj jyj jyj jyyj

Y **words using all known letters**

yes year pay pray yet yard way sway stay

say play joy ploy dry quay eye idly pity

you your sky defy shy grey fly rely tidy

Develop then test accuracy/speed on all known letters

Take that registered letter to the post.
They always like to take a July holiday.
This year we will pay you a good salary.
Twiggy tried quite hard yet just failed.
We defy you to say what you really feet.

. . . . Kdpm

| | | | | | | | |
|5|10|15|20|25|30|35|40|

fTa jkL ;Sf uJk; Yj Ika ;Qej lkFsG HkeL;

Ak Wko Plwp jQrj jY jTopl ;Wfh Il KoDfD;

. . . . Kdpm

Unit 9 Alphabet

Introducing

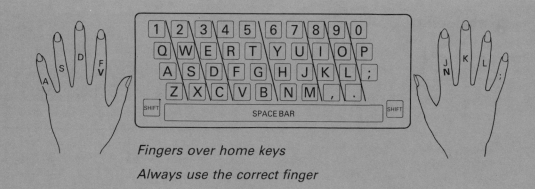

Fingers over home keys

Always use the correct finger

N location drill

● jjn jjn jjn jnn jnn jnn jnj jnj jnj jnnj

N words using all known letters

an any done under join noted until unite ○

in win thin think none grown front spend

no not know known seen queen lines young

V location drill

● ffv ffv ffv fvv fvv fvv fvf fvf fvf fvvf

V words using all known letters

vat vie have gave save wave venue quiver ○

via ivy give live five jive prove valued

vet eve very vast over ever valve revoke

Develop then test accuracy/speed on all known letters

No trains now run to Taunton on Sundays.

She queried the June figures a week ago.

I have never viewed so varied a display.

Every five years the plots are revalued.

Never look on revision as wasted effort.

5	10	15	20	25	30	35	40

.... Kdpm

Dak Kl ;Qfr Juk Vis jNo Pl;sa Gfuky TfRd

dSh Qus vFk kNl; jYd RfE kLp;a Ws Il Hde

.... Kdpm

Unit 10 Alphabet

Introducing

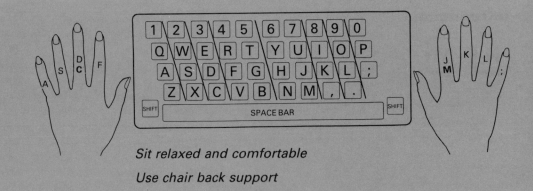

Sit relaxed and comfortable

Use chair back support

M	**location drill**	● jjm jjm jjm jmm jmm jmm jmj jmj jmj jmmj
M	**words using all known letters**	am man men met mark from same name image ◻ me met arm aim harm form jump move madam my may him rim them mine whom some qualm
C	**location drill**	● ddc ddc ddc dcc dcc dcc dcd dcd dcd dccd
C	**words using all known letters**	can car cap cage came which quick accept ◻ ace ice act fact city could check cheque cue cut arc cash jack count clear vacant

Develop then test accuracy/speed on all known letters

Move the summer ball from May to August.
We have not yet received our July quota.
Come in March for the grandfather clock.
In this case you cannot pick and choose.
He is very interested in party politics.

```
|___|___|___|___|___|___|___|___|
    5   10  15  20  25  30  35  40
```

.... Kdpm

jM kSaq lK; fR jUd Gop Trv jN ;Cd Ews Qa
ikO Ysv jMN Rfv Wik Iuh Yjh kGf VcdEA Sk

.... Kdpm

Unit 11 Alphabet

Unit 12 Alphabet

Introducing

and shift lock

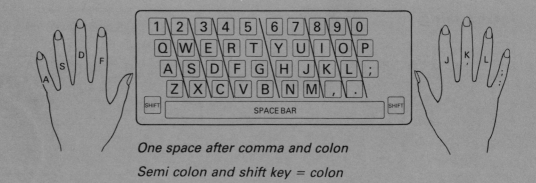

One space after comma and colon

Semi colon and shift key = colon

Shift lock key

This is used to key consecutive capitals.

1 Depress shift lock using little finger of left hand
2 Return left hand to home keys and key the required capitals
3 Release shift lock by depressing either left or right shift key

Testing and recording accuracy/ speed

Add two to your key depressions total for use of shift lock (one for shift lock on, one for shift lock off).

. comma

● kk, kk, kk, k,, k,, k,, k,k k,k k,k k,, k

come, go, stop, wait, see, ask, enquire, ⊙

: colon

● come: go: stop: wait: see: ask: enquire: ⊙

Shift lock

Mum reads THE DAILY MAIL, Dad THE TIMES.

Come on MONDAY, not TUESDAY as arranged.

That cat could NOT have done the damage.

Develop then test accuracy/speed on all known letters

Check your account: it is now OVERDRAWN.

Please take the Minutes of that meeting.

I require pen, pencil, paper and eraser.

In summer, Jim Green likes to play golf.

Never hurry work; more haste less speed.

```
L___L___L___L___L___L___L___L
    5   10   15   20   25   30   35   40
```

.... Kdpm

sAj kI lpO ;Ef Ghy nMj dVfeR Yl; :lO jP;

Dcfi0 UjfG jHy Yv fRl;mN IkMe fEwdW jP:;

.... Kdpm

Unit 12 Alphabet

Introducing

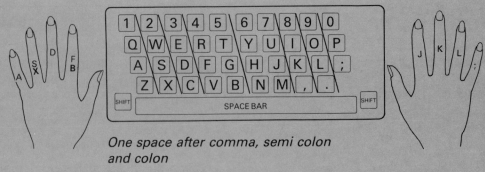

One space after comma, semi colon and colon

Two spaces after full stop

B location drill

⦿ ffb ffb ffb fbb fbb fbb fbf fbf fbf fbbf

B words using all known letters

bad ban bar bag verb robe barber problem ⊙

big but buy bus bark bush double quibble

job mob rob bow able best feeble because

X location drill

⦿ ssx ssx ssx sxx sxx sxx sxs sxs sxs sxxs

X words using all known letters

axe tax wax exit klaxon excite exquisite ⊙

six fix mix exam oxygen exhort excessive

box cox vex apex excuse exodus juxtapose

Develop then test accuracy/speed on all known letters

Alan calls this his black box of tricks.

Both those goods trains made quick time.

I just CANNOT find that expensive watch.

The bank will be open by about February.

Yes: export sales exceeded expectations.

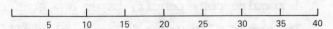

```
    5    10   15   20   25   30   35   40
```

dCdfO jJui Ml sSwf ;Xdp bBkyY Un,s WvfVF

dXi kOl fBr Truy WxQ; :hcE sX, uTg hGoP;

.... Kdpm

.... Kdpm

Unit 13 Alphabet

Introducing

Z

and useful drills

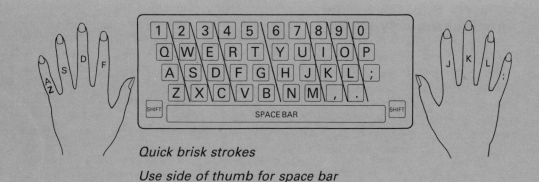

Quick brisk strokes

Use side of thumb for space bar

When you have completed your accuracy/speed testing and recording, practise the alphabet and other drills given — building up accuracy, speed and fluency on each one.

Z **location drill**

⊙aaz aaz aaz azz azz azz aza aza aza azza

Z **words using all letters**

jazz amaze dozen zephyr bizarre frenzied ◻

quiz vizor sizes zodiac zoology kingsize

whiz crazy zebra zenith agonize exorcize

Develop then test accuracy/speed on all letters

Just one more delay invokes the penalty.
If we go, let it be in a blaze of glory.
I expect QUICK returns from investments.
The jazz band played some amazing music.
No: concert tickets were printed in May.

. . . . Kdpm

```
|    |    |    |    |    |    |    |    |
   5   10   15   20   25   30   35   40
```

aZa jkL ;OsW QgnkM kIdEc ;JpQ: jVrTh uIk

XsoP GwOl, fGrRt lUeWv aSxzO; bBmol WxcC

. . . . Kdpm

Alphabetic build-up (continue and cover whole alphabet)

abc abc abc abc abc abc abc abc abc abc
abcd abcd abcd abcd abcd abcd abcd abcd
abcde abcde abcde abcde abcde abcde abcd

Alternate hand words

ass hull bad ill cafe junk deed kill are
nook read oil safe poll tea upon vase in

Alphabet and space bar

a b c d e f g h i j k l m n o p q r s t
u v w x y z a b c d e f g h i j k l m n

Shift lock

Key ACCURATELY and FLUENTLY

Closed capitals (1 space between words)

CORRECTING ERRORS REDUCES SPEED

Spaced capitals (3 spaces between words)

K E Y   V E R Y   A C C U R A T E L Y

Unit 14 Alphabet consolidation

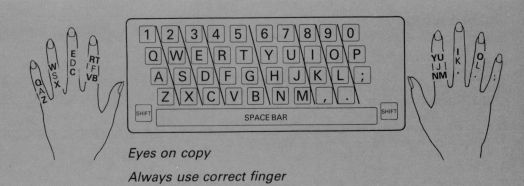

Introducing 3 types of paragraph

Eyes on copy

Always use correct finger

Instructions

Set your machine for a 40-character line as usual.
Copy *line by line* in single spacing, leaving one line of space between paragraphs.
Key each type of paragraph at least twice to improve accuracy, speed and fluency.

Blocked paragraphs

You can now touch key the whole alphabet
as well as important punctuation marks.

These are blocked paragraphs. This
means that all lines of type line up at
the left.

Indented paragraphs

    The first line of an indented
paragraph starts a few spaces to the
right of the other lines. Indentation
must be kept uniform, as here.

    Indented paragraphs are not now as
widely used as blocked ones.

Hanging paragraphs

The third type is known as hanging
  paragraphs. The first line hangs two
  spaces to the left of the others.

Hanging paragraphs are more tricky to
  key. They are seldom used except to
  give a distinctive effect.

Develop then test accuracy/speed on all known letters

Just one official may take leave in May.

In that job I operated a word processor.

Henry has a working knowledge of French.

In hazy mist, Brixton Square was lovely.

CODE: black for this year; red for last.

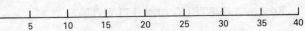

| 5 | 10 | 15 | 20 | 25 | 30 | 35 | 40 |

.... Kdpm

sAz lKf; dEoP; Jwcbk: jHn, fGrT kNb. Ik;

sDgwV lKuM; dVtT jY,: lNiU sQa. dXex fB;

.... Kdpm

22

Unit 15 Figures

Introducing all-figure strings

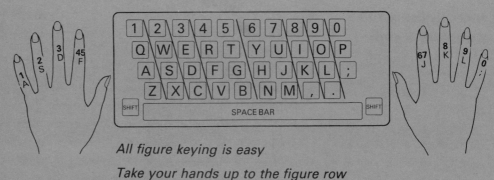

All figure keying is easy

Take your hands up to the figure row

Figures

Place your fingers over the figures row, little fingers on 1 and 0, with 5 and 6 'free' in the middle. Then practise the 4 lines of figure drills.

Testing and recording accuracy/speed

From now on a continuous paragraph is given in each unit for one-minute timing of kdpm as before. Syllabic intensity (SI) measures the average number of syllables per word, and is a measure of difficulty. In the paragraphs SI is kept within the average difficulty range of 1.36 to 1.41 — so you can compare your performance on the different paragraphs.

Use 2 and/or 3 minute timings on the sentences above the numbered bar and on the figure and alphanumeric strings below the bar. 99% accuracy is still required. This means you count your total key depressions up to the 3rd uncorrected error for 200+ kd, and up to the 4th uncorrected error for 300+ kd — and so on. Then divide by 2 or 3 as appropriate to record your kdpm in the boxes provided.

⊡ 111 222 333 444 555 666 777 888 999 0000

000 999 888 777 666 555 444 333 222 1111

104 382 705 760 981 293 786 440 290 7821 ▢

1023 58997 56001 32984 78096 231 66 0032

One-minute a/s paragraph (*SI 1.36*)

Please support the traders who advertise in this programme. Only with their help can we produce it at its very low price.

_____

.... Kdpm

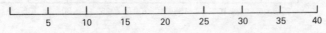

5	10	15	20	25	30	35	40

Develop then test accuracy/speed on all letters then all figures

This year we will pay you a good salary.

In that case you cannot pick and choose.

We will then publish the latest figures.

PRESENT: chairman, secretary, treasurer.

It was just an extremely difficult quiz.

That makes your image quite progressive.

5	10	15	20	25	30	35	40

	2 mins	3 mins
	.... Kdpm	.... Kdpm
	.... Kdpm	.... Kdpm

1209 44 852 00238 98743 22094 118673 248

78450 21 118865 4320 99785 210 009 64503

23

Unit 15A   Figures

Unit 15   Figures

Introducing the numeric keypad

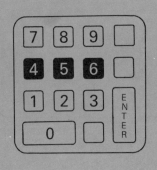 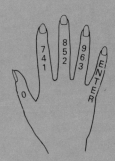

Some machines have a numeric keypad to the right of the main keyboard, for inputting large amounts of all-figure data at speed. If your machine has a figure keypad, work this additional unit; then use the keypad for all-figure strings in future units as an alternative to taking your hands up to the figure row on the main keyboard.

The home keys are 4 5 6 (shaded in the above keypad diagram) and fingering as shown on the hand diagram, the thumb striking 0, and the little finger ENTER (for space).

Key each line at least twice.

```
444 555 666 456 456 654 455 566 645 4655
544 455 644 655 564 645 446 554 664 4566
```

```
447 441 774 114 440 004 470 410 147 1400
456 476 650 457 640 005 505 416 157 1044
```

```
558 552 885 225 285 528 582 255 855 5822
580 246 478 158 602 670 002 808 761 4286
```

```
669 663 996 336 693 669 336 639 963 6399
409 317 283 943 625 341 903 843 276 9032
```

One-minute a/s paragraph (SI 1.39)

Adverts should reach our office by close
of business on Friday in order to appear
in the next weekly issue of the Gazette.

```
|____|____|____|____|____|____|____|
    5   10   15   20   25   30   35   40
```

.... Kdpm

Develop then test a/s on all-figure strings

001 34896 75420 33 8774 3120 679 300 841
22 49786 07 883 219 942 654078 99 232 08

```
|____|____|____|____|____|____|____|
    5   10   15   20   25   30   35   40
```

.... Kdpm

Unit 16 Figures

Introducing

1 2

Always use top row key
for figure one
Check your keying of figures one by
one

When figures and letters are intermixed, figures must be keyed from
the home row. They are now thus introduced, two per unit — with
of course the same fingering as in Unit 15.

Notes (4th line from bottom) The full stop is used to divide hours from
minutes with the 12-hour clock. With the 24-hour clock, 1.22 pm would
be expressed as 1322 hrs (or hours)
All-figure strings below par — take your hands up to the figure row.

1
aa1 aa1 aa1 a11 a11 a11 a1a a1a a1a a11a

aqua 11 alpha 111 agenda 1111 addenda 11

We won 11 and lost 11 matches; 11 drawn.

2
ss2 ss2 ss2 s22 s22 s22 s2s s2s s2s s22s

sobs 22 slips 222 sauces 2222 stones 222

In 2 years I spent 222 days in 22 towns.

**One-minute a/s
paragraph (*SI 1.38*)**

Bad habits are very hard to break. With
a skill like keyboarding it is therefore
important to start with good techniques.

| 5   10   15   20   25   30   35   40 |

.... Kdpm

The AGENDA must be sent out by Thursday.

Jean is simply expert, but far too lazy.

I look forward to hearing from you soon.

You can buy it from any good bookseller.

**Develop then test
accuracy/speed on all
letters and figures 1 and 2**

Simply say the square root of 121 is 11.

I arrived at 1.22 pm, only minutes late.

| 5   10   15   20   25   30   35   40 |

	2 mins	3 mins
	.... Kdpm	.... Kdpm
	.... Kdpm	.... Kdpm

22904 668 34877 01 220 55698 33887 7 616

304 110 02 34987 10788 33661 11 399 0458

sAd2 jklH22 11dEr Td21 uYio 11 12Cxv 21j

Unit 17 Figures

Introducing

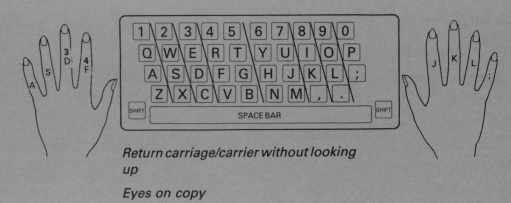

Return carriage/carrier without looking up

Eyes on copy

Notes   (line 6) With the 12-hour clock, am and pm are often omitted when they are known.
Remember to take your hands up to the figures row for all-figure copy below the second bar.

3
```
dd3 dd3 dd3 d33 d33 d33 d3d d3d d3d d33d
dated 33 dared 333 dived 3333 divided 33
Route 33 runs 333 km through the valley.
```

4
```
ff4 ff4 ff4 f44 f44 f44 f4f f4f f4f f44f
fluff 4 far off 44 frilly cuff 4 fluff 4
The 4.44 express is now 44 minutes late.
```

All known figures
```
34 ties, 43 chairs, 123 pans, 432 brooms
413 cups, 243 plates, 124 cows, 431 pigs
```

One-minute a/s paragraph (*SI 1.39*)
```
It is not hard for most of us to achieve
high speed and accuracy at the keyboard.
Use the correct fingers and concentrate.
```
.... Kdpm

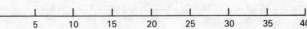
```
  5    10   15   20   25   30   35   40
```

Develop then test accuracy/speed on all letters and all known figures
```
Please send them your latest price list.
He has the gift for figures that I lack.
They then saw him quickly close the box.
My annual turnover is considerably down.
Jilly knocked 12 SECONDS off the record.
A group of 34 researchers went to Zaire.
```

	2 mins	3 mins
	.... Kdpm	.... Kdpm
	.... Kdpm	.... Kdpm

```
  5    10   15   20   25   30   35   40
```

```
441 3006 87 9678 00346 22114 229 88 3376
303 22 80096 424 220 45912 07780 39887 2
fFhk34 1342V kJi44 Cdsa112 443Fb B331 S3
```

Unit 18   Figures

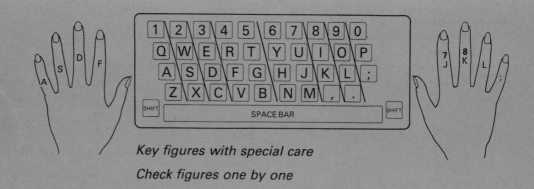

Key figures with special care

Check figures one by one

Notes   (line 3) The full stop is used for the decimal point.
(line 8) The comma can be used as thousand marker in figures
of 4 or more digits.

7

jj7 jj7 jj7 j77 j77 j77 j7j j7j j7j j77j

guru 77 jets in situ 777 jugs of pilau 7

In 7 days I drove 777 miles at 77.7 mph.

8

kk8 kk8 kk8 k88 k88 k88 k8k k8k k8k k88k

kick 88 knack 888 knock 8888 knapsack 88

On 8 August, Flight 88 leaves at 8.8 pm.

All known figures

217 cats, 128 dots, 437 sums, 823 tables

387 figs, 14 tops, 874 caps, 12,438 bars

One-minute a/s paragraph (*SI 1.36*)

Best prices paid for all antiques. When
you realise the value of the ring auntie
left, you might get a pleasant surprise.

. . . . Kdpm

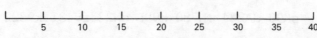

```
   5    10    15    20    25    30    35    40
```

Develop then test accuracy/speed on all letters and all known figures

You promised to send them before Friday.
The new bank will do very good business.
Please ring me at home just before noon.
My class must work EXTRA HARD this term.
Queenie and Zoe scored 38 and 47 points.
My brothers are now 17 and 24 years old.

```
   5    10    15    20    25    30    35    40
```

27789 12506 118 33694 02137 1289547 8891

200458 6600923 5890 449 128 0022875 7 66

843B 77adE 2143F jJ778 12438 sX227 ik874

	2 mins	3 mins
	. . . . Kdpm	. . . . Kdpm
	. . . . Kdpm	. . . . Kdpm

Unit 19   Figures

Introducing

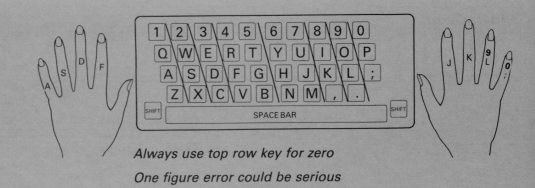

Always use top row key for zero

One figure error could be serious

9

119 119 119 199 199 199 191 191 191 1991
lull 99 level 999 local 9999 lintel 9999
I dialled 999 as 99 people were injured.

0

;;0 ;;0 ;;0 ;00 ;00 ;00 ;0; ;0; ;0; ;00;
Nil may be expressed as 0, 0.0, or 0.00.

All known figures

100 fads, 289 hats, 437 jigs, 2,390 peas
244 goats, 379 pigs, 801 cows, 197 sheep

One-minute a/s paragraph (*SI 1.37*)

Modern life is so routine, it is natural
at times to feel that we are merely cogs
in a wheel. Creative hobbies rescue us.

.... Kdpm

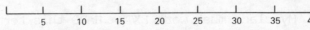

Develop then test accuracy/speed on all letters and all known figures

I told you we were out of stock of them.
Most prices will rise sharply next year.
I take a large size in shoes and gloves.
Yes, their profit margin is now TOO LOW.
Granny lived to the ripe old age of 109.
Jim used 2,348 tacks in 72 square boxes.

	2 mins	3 mins
	.... Kdpm	.... Kdpm
	.... Kdpm	.... Kdpm

2003 4897 113 40028 7784 40 001287 79931
94001 223 0078 114430 228 917 007722 448
sK90 dA224 mN780 k99L dW23 fV431 k9322 0

Unit 20 Figures

Introducing

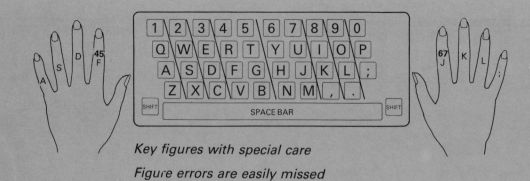

Key figures with special care

Figure errors are easily missed

Note (line 6) 'Number' abbreviated to 'No'

5

ff5 ff5 ff5 f55 f55 f55 f5f f5f f5f f55f
fluff 5 far off 55 frilly cuff 5 fluff 5
After 5 minutes, at 5.55, I saw 55 cabs.

6

jj6 jj6 jj6 j66 j66 j66 j6j j6j j6j j66j
guru 66 jets in situ 666 jugs of pilau 6
Their flat is No 66 at 66 Pine Row, NW6.

All figures

560 sums, 128 dots, 349 peas, 5,704 hats
122 lids, 346 figs, 897 bars, 605 cables

One-minute a/s paragraph (*SI 1.39*)

I have made up my mind that I shall keep
my diary more efficiently. I must write
in all engagements and details promptly.

. . . . Kdpm

```
|    |    |    |    |    |    |    |    |
     5   10   15   20   25   30   35   40
```

Develop then test accuracy/speed on all letters and all known figures

We shall have to raise prices in August.
Sit by an exit so you can leave quickly.
We MUST keep down the cost of overheads.
Tomorrow, Wednesday, is publication day.
297 young Japs died in the blazing vans.
On 15 May we sold 360 books and 48 maps.

```
|    |    |    |    |    |    |    |    |
     5   10   15   20   25   30   35   40
```

	2 mins	3 mins
	. . . . Kdpm	. . . . Kdpm
	. . . . Kdpm	. . . . Kdpm

20045 668 91670 44 6083 312 5687 9900455
49100 007 8452 38096 966 45001 238045 81
jN905 dsC43 11V hY890 j7621 11K 2256F 56

Unit 21 Figures consolidation

**Introducing
simple tabulation**

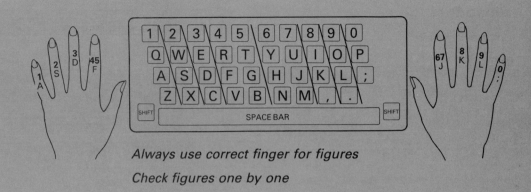

Always use correct finger for figures

Check figures one by one

Set your machine for a 40 line-length as usual.
Set first tabulator stop 10 spaces to the right of left margin.
Set second tab stop 10 spaces to the right of first tab stop.
Set third tab stop 10 spaces to the right of second tab stop.
Follow the layout given, working *across* the columns using a ruler as a guide.
Copy at least twice.

(*Electronic machines*: use the decimal tabulator, if available, to automatically align the decimal points.)

NUMBER	CODE	PRICE	TOTAL
10	24.18	22.56	225.60
8	48.10	24.60	196.80
15	84.06	9.85	147.75
7	36.72	18.70	130.90
12	15.24	9.25	111.00
8	53.67	6.75	54.00
14	12.85	12.50	175.00

**One-minute a/s
paragraph (*SI 1.40*)**

Always be relaxed at your keyboard, feet
firmly on the floor, and back supported.
Sitting screwed up brings painful aches.

.... Kdpm

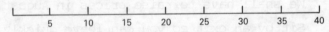

**Develop then test
accuracy/speed on all
letters and all figures**

We CANNOT deliver them before next week.

Entries must be in by the end of August.

They expect very good results this year.

If we go, let it be in a blaze of glory.

Our train is due at 1450 hours on 6 May.

Jane Rix moved from 28 to 379 Quay Walk.

	2 mins	3 mins
	.... Kdpm	.... Kdpm
	.... Kdpm	.... Kdpm

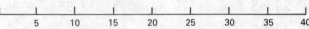

775 2001 268 0088743 6621 002 55229 3704

448 993461 5 33012 11880 76698 003 20 88

dA45 jj670 44 sQ11 kI908 fV675 kU543 e31

Units 22-30 Extra punctuation and symbols

Location of these signs and symbols

Although the location of letters and figures is standard on all QWERTY keyboards, this is no longer so with extra punctuation and symbols. Different manufacturers have different arrangements for them. From now on you should use the keyboard chart supplied with this book, after filling in the extra punctuation and symbols as they appear on your keyboard.

Before you practise the location drills in Units 22–29, neatly write through each dot the controlling home key as shown on the keyboard chart. In every case you use the appropriate figure finger or the nearer little finger. For example, if the asterisk key is over the figure 1 and therefore struck with the left little finger, the location drill (the pattern you are already familar with) will appear as:

aa* aa* aa* a** a** a** a*a a*a a*a a**a

Testing and recording accuracy/speed

A one-minute accuracy/speed paragraph will continue to be given in each Unit for testing as before.

In the **Extra punctuation section** (Units 22–25) the sentences above the numbered bar should be tested over 5 or 7 minutes, dividing your total key depressions (as previously counted) by 5 or 7 to find your kdpm. The figure strings, etc, below the bar should be timed over 3 or 4 minutes. (Remember, if you finish within the time, start again.)

In the **Symbols section** (Units 26–29) increase your timing on the sentences to 8 or 10 minutes, keeping the figure strings, etc, to 3 or 4 minutes.

Information processing definitions

From Unit 22 onwards you should start to practise (and record results) the paragraphs given in Appendix A on pages 43 to 48.

Unit 22 Extra punctuation

Introducing

$\boxed{-}$

hyphen and dash

$\boxed{-}$ **location drill**   ..– ..– ..– .–– .–– .–– .–. .–. .–. .–. .––.

Hyphen

hit-or-miss, up-to-date, happy-go-lucky,
re-enter, re-elected, co-operated, Co-op
84GWS-48AB BK11-382YG AD44-265Z VAX-B214

Dash

up – not down, me – not him, 12 – not 13
she – not he – won; he – not she – paid;

One-minute a/s paragraph (SI 1.39)

A freak blizzard cut off a major port in
Kent last night. Police said that Dover
was in absolute chaos after an hour-long
storm, with a number of fatal accidents.

```
  |____|____|____|____|____|____|____|
       5    10   15   20   25   30   35   40
```

.... Kdpm

Develop then test accuracy/speed on all letters, all figures and all known punctuation

The new printing works opened last June.

Your plan will ensure a big improvement.

No; Ray cannot give enough time to work.

See the mid-term result – OUR BEST EVER.

The train is now due at 1835, Zena says.

Cheque No. 024769 is faulty: explain it.

```
  |____|____|____|____|____|____|____|
       5    10   15   20   25   30   35   40
```

5 mins	7 mins
.... Kdpm	.... Kdpm

220 18946 77802 44 956 66003 22 10 31789
4456 409 9002 77 90 00125 2004578 987756
22-34 6AB-89XZ 776aA 1590B-M jKl20-24 fF

3 mins	4 mins
.... Kdpm	.... Kdpm

Unit 23 Extra punctuation

Introducing

single and double quotes

The apostrophe is always used to show possession and omission of letter(s): see lines 2 and 3.

In other uses, single and double quotes are interchangeable as follows:
a   Direct speech — see lines 4 and 7
b   Special use of word(s) — see lines 5 and 8
c   Quotes within quotes — see lines 9 and 10

single quote or apostrophe

1   ..' ..' ..' .'' .'' .'' .'. .'. .'. .''.

2   Mary's kitten tore all the girls' coats.

3   He hadn't the strength and I didn't try.

4   'I have told the truth', said the youth.

5   She was the 'prima donna' of the school.

double quotes

6   .." .." .." ."" ."" ."" ."." ."." ."." ."".

7   "I have told the truth", said the youth.

8   She was the "prima donna" of the school.

9   I said "He called 'Let go' and ran off".

10   I said 'He called "Let go" and ran off'.

For feet and inches

6' 8", 24' 10", 15' 9", 10' 8" diameter,

One-minute a/s paragraph (*SI 1.41*)

Last summer more people than ever took a holiday abroad. Most chose places where they could count on sunshine. But there was a big rise also in adventure travel.

| 5   10   15   20   25   30   35   40 |

.... Kdpm

Develop then test accuracy/speed on all letters, all figures and all known punctuation

All our queries were full of good ideas.

Jim speaks French; Pam knows some Greek.

The concert - for once - was a sell-out.

"I wrote to 'The Times' today", he said.

No: 650 boxes of 3 dozen were delivered.

Her father was born on 27 DECEMBER 1948.

| 5   10   15   20   25   30   35   40 |

5 mins	7 mins
.... Kdpm	.... Kdpm

210 348967 5502 307634 77 2003 006 79865

33 4005 667891 22076 55 3 4578 99931 110

60-79 sAdB4-6 9'10"-12'6" fV33 275 SA-Zb

3 mins	4 mins
.... Kdpm	.... Kdpm

Unit 24 Extra punctuation

Introducing

? **(question mark)**

..? ..? ..? .?? .?? .?? .?. .?. .?. ..??.
Who? What? When? Where? Why? Which?
May I? Why not? Is he sure? Will you?

((brackets)
)

..(..(..(.((.((.((.(. .(. .(. .((.
..) ..) ..) .)) .)) .)) .). .). .). .)).
(2 cows) (4 pigs) (65 goats) (138 sheep)
(Code X300) (24.1.86) (2000 cc) (Age 26)

One-minute a/s paragraph (SI 1.41)

This city has been important since Roman times, yet it is keeping up with today's needs. Both work and leisure facilities have grown, to make a noted arts centre.

.... Kdpm

| | 5 | 10 | 15 | 20 | 25 | 30 | 35 | 40 |

Develop then test accuracy/speed on all letters, all figures and all known punctuation

Fanny, enquire about our hotel expenses.
Vic Boxhall is NOT lazy; everyone knows.
Listen: Mr Jay (not Mr Kay) speaks next.
"I read 'The Guardian' today", she said.
No - they meant the 15-storey buildings.
Can you ring me on 24679 before 8.30 pm?

| | 5 | 10 | 15 | 20 | 25 | 30 | 35 | 40 |

5 mins	7 mins
.... Kdpm	.... Kdpm

3 mins	4 mins
.... Kdpm	.... Kdpm

002 33987 6651 883 00213 773412 889 7677
200 44 5 67980 2143 66 90863 2690 338899
3'10"-5'4"(D-K) fGdE(37) (100)WQ 88-99 V

Unit 25 Extra punctuation consolidation

Set your machine for a 40 line-length as usual.
Copy line by line, carefully following the layout and styling given.
Copy at least twice — until you can key it accurately, quickly and fluently.
Note use of the hyphen to divide words at line-ends (division always between syllables).

```
CHANNEL ISLANDS GILT FUND LIMITED

Do you wish to earn 12.7 per cent immed-
iate income?  You can do so by investing
in Gilts with us.  Note these points:-

(1)  THE FUND - primarily invests in
     "exempt" British Government Securi-
     ties (Gilts).  These are Gilts
     which are not liable to any UK tax-
     ation.

(2)  QUARTERLY DIVIDENDS - paid free of
     any witholding taxes.

(3)  NO FIXED TERM - the investment can
     be held for as long as you wish.

(4)  MINIMUM INVESTMENT - one thousand
     pounds.
```

One-minute a/s paragraph (*SI 1.39*)

```
This firm needs a fast and accurate male
or female keyboard operator.  We can pay
a high salary to the right person.  Call
us at once if you meet our requirements.
```

.... Kdpm

```
 |    |    |    |    |    |    |    |
      5   10   15   20   25   30   35   40
```

Develop then test accuracy/speed on all letters, all figures and all known punctuation

```
Will your plan ensure a big improvement?

I told Mr John (the manager) of my fear.

I need a plan - not a short-term remedy.

The size is not crucial; the quality is.

"This story by 'Saki' is VERY suitable."

We arrived at 9.27, just 4 minutes late.

Rex moved to 68 King Street, tel: 53001.
```

5 mins	7 mins
.... Kdpm	.... Kdpm

```
 |    |    |    |    |    |    |    |
      5   10   15   20   25   30   35   40
```

```
22 34500 11987 66 589034 21 336987 00443

100 38976 556 4409 2093 44 6 8895 776044

(94-98) 2AfJ34 4'7"-12'9" (99) BAZ(4317)
```

3 mins	4 mins
.... Kdpm	.... Kdpm

Unit 26 Symbols

Introducing

Notes @ sign (at) is used mainly in invoices and similar documents.
(line 5) Small letter p is used as an abbreviation for 'pence' in amount
of money consisting of pence only. For amounts of mixed pounds
and pence, the £ sign and decimal point are always used.

**Testing and
recording accuracy/
speed**

Always start again if you finish before the timing is up.

£ (pound sign)

```
..£. ..£. ..£. .££. .££. .££. .£. .£. .£. .££.
pay £8, give £7, ask £5, take £36, at £2
Rooms cost £40 and meals from £9 to £15.
```

@ ('at' sign)

```
..@. ..@. ..@. .@@. .@@. .@@. .@. .@. .@. .@@.
@ 65p, @ 78p, @ 94p, @59p, @ 20p, @ 13p
Buy pears @ 87p and nuts @ 95p per kilo.
```

**One-minute a/s
paragraph (*SI 1.36*)**

```
Have you ever thought how exciting it is
on those first days of the year when the
weather is hot enough for summer attire?
Life seems altogether brighter, all your
cares discarded like the winter clothes.
```
      5   10   15   20   25   30   35   40

.... Kdpm

**Develop then test
accuracy/speed on all
letters, all figures, all
punctuation and all
known symbols**

```
Please draft a polite letter of refusal.
Yes, their profit margin is now too low.
Not knowing, can we just hazard a guess?
Verdict on end-of-quarter results - bad.
CODE: C for cars (or vans); B for buses.
"I've explained all that quite clearly."
My staff of 180 includes 46 secretaries.
Buy 13 pillows @ £9, and 27 covers @ £5.
```
      5   10   15   20   25   30   35   40

	8 mins	10 mins
	.... Kdpm	.... Kdpm

	3 mins	4 mins
	.... Kdpm	.... Kdpm

```
330 1289765 2 66 77031 658902 448661 999
02 1004 57689 23091 93355 61128 002 3006
A219 784CE £653-£712 (Cat 329) 4 @ £7.65
```

Unit 27 Symbols

Introducing

%	*

Notes   % sign (per cent) is used only with figures (10%, but ten per cent **or** 10 per cent.
The asterisk * and ** can be used for footnotes as an alternative to raised (superscript) figures.

% (per cent)

..% ..% ..% .%% .%% .%% .%. .%. .%. .%%.
over 10%, under 25%, pay 7%, 8% interest
Results of 90%, 80% and 55% average 75%.

* (asterisk)

..* ..* ..* .** .** .** .*. .*. .*. .**.
red* blue* green* yellow* orange* black*
Sizes* and prices** below, as indicated.

One-minute a/s paragraph (*SI 1.38*)

We all have interests and talents of one
kind or other, which as a rule are akin.
We need to succeed in what interests us,
and fully utilise all those talents. By
working hard at it, rewards will follow.

```
|___|___|___|___|___|___|___|___|
    5   10  15  20  25  30  35  40
```

.... Kdpm

Develop then test accuracy/speed on all letters, all figures, all punctuation and all known symbols

You can buy it from any good bookseller.
Jack is quite expert – but is very lazy.
Can you ring her at home, about mid-day?
The need is for (a) accuracy; (b) speed.
"We're all over here", Harry called out.
Order today to obtain our 10% discount*.
Mary knocked 2.3 SECONDS off the record.
Buy the table @ £487 and 6 chairs @ £95.

```
|___|___|___|___|___|___|___|___|
    5   10  15  20  25  30  35  40
```

8 mins	10 mins
.... Kdpm	.... Kdpm

11 20 4489 2398685 330 002 446785 997564
006 773399 21104 89673 9002448 7769453 2
3'10"–4'7" 12 @ £8.50 (Cat 2967B) 43 10%*

3 mins	4 mins
.... Kdpm	.... Kdpm

Unit 28 Symbols

Introducing

& (ampersand)

```
..& ..& ..& .&& .&& .&& .&. .&. .&. .&&.
Mr & Mrs, May 7 & 8, Day & Son, Rae & Co
Ross & Hardy incorporated Hardy & Jones.
```

/ (solidus)

```
../ ../ ../ .// .// .// ./. ./. ./. .//.
Mr/Mrs/Miss, him/her, I/we, cash/cheque;
Write/phone Ure Bros, 48/50 High Street.
```

One-minute a/s paragraph (*SI 1.40*)

Travel with us to Via, a modern purpose-built resort perched high amid scenes of grandeur in the Italian Alps. There are privilege rates for small children. For full details, return the coupon at once.

```
  |    |    |    |    |    |    |    |
       5   10   15   20   25   30   35   40
```

.... Kdpm

Develop then test accuracy/speed on all letters, all figures, all punctuation and all known symbols

Please telephone me as soon as possible.
Annual turnover was bad: very much down.
Entries should be in by the end of July.
Bye-laws - and local custom - forbid it.
"Has Vic arrived?" John's brother asked.
Make it in (1) pink; (2) azure; (3) tan.
Clark & Green are at 58/64 Exton Square.
Purchase 7 @ £9, to get a 10% DISCOUNT*.

```
  |    |    |    |    |    |    |    |
       5   10   15   20   25   30   35   40
```

330 298567 110 204 33654789 2109 8844321
2 44 6003 007 33097546 2112 30456 890754
ASK/ew 2198 & 456rT 25% 22 @ £76.95 5'8"

	8 mins	10 mins
	.... Kdpm	.... Kdpm

	3 mins	4 mins
	.... Kdpm	.... Kdpm

Unit 29 Symbols

Introducing mathematical and scientific symbols

Use small or capital letter x (follow copy) for the multiplication sign, and a hyphen for the minus sign. Always follow precisely the spacing in the copy.

⊡ (equals sign)

..= ..= ..= .== .== .== .=. .=. .=. .==.
9 x 8 = 72   12 x 12 = 144   6 x 2 - 3 = 9

⊞ (plus sign)

..+ ..+ ..+ .++ .++ .++ .+. .+. .+. .++.
7 + 9 = 16   19 + 8 = 27   22 - 5 + 9 = 26

Scientific symbols (2 spaces between columns)

Ca (calcium)	Pb (lead)	Na (sodium)
C (carbon)	O (oxygen)	Sn (tin)
Au (gold)	K (potassium)	U (uranium)
Fe (iron)	Ag (silver)	Zn (zinc)

One-minute a/s paragraph (*SI 1.40*)

Clearly the Government does not think it would be wise to reduce taxes this year. At the same time, it is commonly thought that some stimulus to the economy is now required. So public spending may go up.

.... Kdpm

```
 |   |    |    |    |    |    |    |
 5   10   15   20   25   30   35   40
```

Develop then test accuracy/speed on all letters, all figures, all punctuation and all known symbols

Please ring me at home just before noon.
They are very expert: but much too lazy.
The lowest quote was from Redman & Son*.
No - a HALF-TERM report on his/her work.
Call now (today), or next week (Monday).
"What's that? I just don't believe it."
Take a load of our logs @ £19; save 15%.
Cheque 06417823 went astray in the post.

8 mins	10 mins
.... Kdpm	.... Kdpm

```
 |   |    |    |    |    |    |    |
 5   10   15   20   25   30   35   40
```

100 339876 33 45678 00216 7786 99443 220
22 9063 5698768 0023 300 11 2034985 55 3
12 - 8 = 4   10 x 12 = 120   4 x 3 - 4 = 8
8 + 6 = 14   18 + 9 = 27   25 - 4 + 8 = 29

3 mins	4 mins
.... Kdpm	.... Kdpm

Text containing all letters, all figures and most symbols

Set yor machine for a 40 line-length as usual.
Copy the text line by line, as shown — at least twice.
Set a tab stop at 1" for discount, VAT and TOTAL.
Also set a tab stop for the start of the money column

We reject your claim that Invoice No Z87
is correct. Working from your catalogue
and price list, the cost of the items is
made up exactly as follows:-

```
24 chairs @ £85 (Cat No 82)        2,040.00

          - 5% discount              102.00
                                   _____

                                   £1,938.00
                                   _____


6 tables @ £150 (Cat No 776)         900.00

          - 5% discount               45.00
                                   _____

                                    £855.00
                                   _____


Both items together                2,793.00

          + VAT @ 15%                418.95
                                   _____

          TOTAL                   £3,211.95
                                   _____
```

On the question of belated complaint, we
would refer you to our Trade Associa-
tion's booklet on Business Practice*,
which takes account of the Stevens &
Johnson Report on this matter.

* Published by Jenners.

One minute a/s paragraph (*SI 1.40*)

We have just opened a large new showroom
in the Bourne shopping centre. Come and
see our wide selection of kitchen equipment. Take advantage of our big opening
discounts for the best bargains in town.

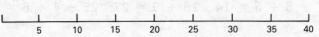

```
|   |    |    |    |    |    |    |    |
5   10   15   20   25   30   35   40
```

006 229984 6785980 0118 009 30 56879 331

44 001 23985674 66 220 881196754 3300 18

AJS/mk 45 @ £10.50 30% (Cat 349B) 22&45*

.... Kdpm

	3 mins	4 mins
	.... Kdpm	.... Kdpm

Unit 31

Introducing computer programs

Computer programs are sets of machine instructions, written in a computer language (BASIC, COBAL, FORTRAN, etc). They are written by computer programmers.

The following section of a computer program is written in BASIC. Copy it exactly at least twice.

```
100 PRINT "STOCK MAINTENANCE OPTIONS"
200 PRINT "SELECT ONE OF THE FOLLOWING"
300 PRINT "        1 FILE HEADER CHANGES"
400 PRINT "        2 ADDITIONS OF NEW ITEMS"
500 PRINT "        3 CHANGES TO EXISTING ITEMS"
600 PRINT "        4 PRICE & DISCOUNT CHANGES"
700 PRINT "ENTER REQUIRED SELECTION" : INPUT A
800 IF A=1 THEN GOTO 1200
810 IF A=2 THEN GOTO 1300
820 IF A=3 THEN GOTO 1400
830 IF A=4 THEN GOTO 1500
900 PRINT "INVALID SELECTION - TRY AGAIN"
920 GOTO 700
```

One minute a/s paragraph (SI 1.36)

This company has had a highly successful year, with profits well up on last year. Our results in most sectors compare well with those of our competitors. If costs are kept down, our prospects are bright.

```
    |   |   |   |   |   |   |   |
        5   10  15  20  25  30  35  40
```

. . . . Kdpm

Develop then test accuracy/speed on all letters, all figures, all punctuation and all known symbols

No, concert tickets were printed in May.

My long-lost friend — Ian Rae — is here.

Will their plan ensure a 7% improvement?

Send cash/cheque* to Sexton & Jefferson.

"So the 'crazy season' is over", I said.

Try it in (1) red; (2) green; (3) black.

Rush out and buy those 5 ties @ £4 each.

Lucky winner of the raffle: TICKET 6089.

```
    |   |   |   |   |   |   |   |
        5   10  15  20  25  30  35  40
```

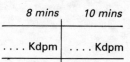

8 mins	10 mins
. . . . Kdpm	. . . . Kdpm

20 1983476 55 340976 44 2001 9856 003 55

002 3399 43210 678954 45002 118 99884 00

26 - 5 + 7 = 28   9 + 7 = 16   17 + 8 = 25

11 - 6 = 5   11 x 11 = 121   5 x 2 - 3 = 7

3 mins	4 mins
. . . . Kdpm	. . . . Kdpm

Unit 32 Simple tabulation

With short, regular tabs like the first two given below, use the space bar twice between columns.

Otherwise set the tab stops at regular intervals (1″, 1½″, 2″, etc) width depending on the copy. In the third tab given below, tab stops are set at 1″ intervals in 12-pitch type.

Copy each tab at least twice.

```
Type  Price  R/V
N/Ag  90.00  105
S/Pr  15.50  387
O/L   46.00  655


No.   Serv  Map
104   SE A  206
216   SE B  193
307   SE C  568

SOUTHERN COUNTIES

Kent       Dorset    Sussex

Devon      Surrey    Hampshire

Cornwall   Somerset  Wiltshire
```

One minute a/s paragraph (*SI 1.39*)

```
Set in its own large landscaped gardens,
the seafront Rock Hotel offers you charm
and luxury, with the highest standard of
service.  It is close to the city shops.
Book summer holiday or short breaks now.
```

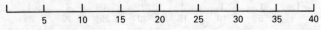

.... Kdpm

Develop then test accuracy/speed on all letters, all figures, all punctuation and all known symbols

```
Coming by train is faster than by coach.
Where?  Is it on a desk, or in a drawer?
Be brief.  Time (and tempers) are short.
My parents - and in-laws - speak Welsh*.
Your plan MUST ensure a 10% improvement.
Flight QX 857 left Jakarta an hour late.
"Last month's orders arrived yesterday."
Zola & Co. 29/34 Kew Row, had them @ £6.
```

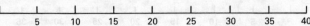

8 mins	10 mins
.... Kdpm	.... Kdpm

```
22 001 45698 88990 34879 22105 44550 223
100 44 8901 298675 4598023 1194780 34127
14%* 3458/1290 (7'2") 238 @ £9.25 Aj&dW2
```

3 mins	4 mins
.... Kdpm	.... Kdpm

Appendix A

Paragraphs defining information processing terms keyed to a 50 line-length. The cumulative kd count to the end of each line is given for each paragraph. Test yourself in timings of 1-5 minutes, recording your kdpm count in the boxes provided.

Use 6-10 minute timings for the full page passage given at the end. If a particular letter/key causes problems, practise the appropriate drill from Appendix B.

	Kd
APPLICATIONS PACKAGE The writing of individual	49
application computer programs and high quality	96
support documentation can be a lengthy and expen-	146
sive exercise. However, in some application	192
areas, eg estate agents and payroll work, good	239
packages already exist, which can either be used	289
as they stand or modified to meet one's needs.	336

. . . . mins

. . . . Kdpm

AUTOMATIC CENTRING of headings, etc, between mar-	51
gins or other designated points is achieved by use	102
of the CENTRE function key.	130

. . . . mins

. . . . Kdpm

AUTOMATIC DECIMAL TABULATOR With this device the	51
operator can key decimal numbers without worrying	101
about alignment of the decimal points: this is	149
done automaticallly by the machine.	184

. . . . mins

. . . . Kdpm

BI-DIRECTIONAL PRINTER When printing from stored	53
text the printer prints out alternate lines back-	103
wards - from right to left - for speed.	143

. . . . mins

. . . . Kdpm

A BLOCK is a portion of text, specified in length	51
by placing block markers at its beginning and end.	102
Text is defined in this way for text-editing pur-	153
poses, eg in the deletion or movement of para-	200
graphs.	208

. . . . mins

. . . . Kdpm

CENTRAL PROCESSING UNIT (CPU) This consists of	49
the three main components of any computer which	97
control processing of data - the memory, the	142
arithmetic unit, and the control unit. The con-	192
trol unit controls the passage of data numbers	239
between the memory and the arithmetic unit: it	287
also detects which arithmetic operation has to be	337
performed, ie it controls use of the instruc-	383
tions.	390

. . . . mins

. . . . Kdpm

DAISY WHEEL PRINT HEAD This is a disc with a ring   52
of spokes radiating like the petals of a daisy.   100
At the tip of each spoke is a character. The disc   153
rotates until the required character is in posi-   202
tion, when a hammer flies out and hits it on to   250
the paper, through a ribbon. Daisy wheels are   298
available in different type styles and sizes and   347
are easily changed over.   372

.... mins
_____
.... Kdpm

DELETION On text-editing equipment, part of a   48
text (eg a letter, word, line or lines) can be re-   101
moved by use of the DELETE function key. A gap is   155
avoided by automatic line adjustment.   193

.... mins
_____
.... Kdpm

A DISCRETIONARY HYPHEN is one used in word divi-   50
sion at the end of a line for appearance sake (ie   101
to lessen the space to be absorbed in justifica-   150
tion or to keep a reasonably even right-hand mar-   200
gin in the normal typing mode). If, with line   249
adjustment during text-editing, the divided word   298
is moved from the end of the line, the discretion-   349
ary hyphen is dropped. See also REQUIRED HYPHEN.   401

.... mins
_____
.... Kdpm

A FOOTER is a short piece of text or other infor-   51
mation that appears at the foot of each page in a   101
document. See also HEADER.   131

FORMAT/FORMATTING A format is the layout of text   51
(margins, page length, justification, etc) decided   104
by the operator. When the text is stored in the mem- 155
ory and later recalled, it will appear as format-   205
ted by the operator. Formats can be changed with-   257
out having to rekey the text.   287

.... mins
_____
.... Kdpm

FUNCTION KEYS on a keyboard are used to control   49
editing, storage, printing, and other processing   98
of text.   107

.... mins
_____
.... Kdpm

	Kd	
HARD COPY is text that is printed on paper - as distinct from 'soft copy' which exists on a screen or on a disc or other storage medium.	49 102 140	. . . . mins —————— . . . . Kdpm
HARDWARE is the tangible machinery of a system as distinct from 'software' - programs, instructions, etc - which control the operation of the hardware.	51 99 147 157	. . . . mins —————— . . . . Kdpm
A HEADER is a short piece of text (eg a heading) or other information (eg a reference) that appears at the top of each page in a document. See also FOOTER.	52 105 155 165	. . . . mins —————— . . . . Kdpm
INFORMATION PROCESSING is a general term covering all computer and word processor operations (editing, sorting, merging, computing, etc) from input to output - for business, mathematical, scientific, or other purposes.	49 96 147 193 224	. . . . mins —————— . . . . Kdpm
INPUT is information entered into a system, the keyboard being the most common method of inputting. OUTPUT is the final result produced by a system, usually by printer on paper.	49 97 147 184	. . . . mins —————— . . . . Kdpm
INSERTION On text-editing equipment, new material (eg a letter, word, line or lines) can be inserted into existing text by use of the INSERT function key. The lines are automatically adjusted as necessary to accommodate the insertion.	52 105 156 208 245	. . . . mins —————— . . . . Kdpm
JUSTIFIED RIGHT-MARGIN means that all lines of text end at the same point. This is achieved by automatic adjustment of the spaces between letters and words.	50 100 151 162	. . . . mins —————— . . . . Kdpm
K is an abbreviation for kilobyte, which is a unit of measurement of memory or storage capacity. A kilobyte is 1024 bytes or characters.	51 101 139	. . . . mins —————— . . . . Kdpm

LIST PROCESSING A list of variable information is 52
created for insertion into a separately created 100
standard document (eg names and addresses into a 150
circular letter). The variables are then automa- 201
tically inserted within the standard document, at 251
designated points (stop codes) during print out. 302
In this way a 'personalised' circular letter is 353

.... mins

produced for each recipient. This process is also 405

known as MERGING. 425

.... Kdpm

MEMORY Part of memory capacity is devoted to 47
storage of software: that part assigned to storage 99
of keyed in text is often called the buffer. This 151
storage is temporary for as soon as electric cur- 201
rent is switched off, the memory's contents dis- 251

.... mins

appear. For more permanent storage the text must 302

be transferred to disc. 326

.... Kdpm

An ORPHAN LINE is the last line of a paragraph 49
which appears by itself at the top of a page. 95
These spoil the appearances of printed text and 143

.... mins

systems can find them and readjust page lengths 191

to get rid of them. See also WIDOW LINE. 235

.... Kdpm

A PROGRAM is a set of machine instructions, 45
written in a computer language (BASIC, COBOL, 93
etc) which are automatically carried out by the 142

.... mins

system in sequence. They are devised by computer 193

programmers. 206

.... Kdpm

A REQUIRED HYPHEN is one that is essential to a 49
compound word (eg self-sufficient) as opposed to 100
a DISCRETIONARY HYPHEN, used only to divide a word 153
at the end of a line. The operator distinguishes 204
between the two so that if lines are adjusted dur- 255

.... mins

ing text-editing, the system retains required 301

hyphens. See also DISCRETIONARY HYPHEN. 344

.... Kdpm

SEARCH AND REPLACE A specified string of charac- 51
ters (eg a name or date) is automatically searched 104
for throughout stored text: and wherever found it 155
is replaced by an alternative specified character 205
string. In this way, recurring errors can be 252 . . . . mins
easily corrected. 270 . . . . Kdpm

SINGLE-STRIKE RIBBON This is a type of carbon 50
ribbon which is good for only one pass through the 101
printer, after which it is discarded and replaced. 152 . . . . mins
It provides the highest quality print. 192 . . . . Kdpm

STOP CODE Stored text (eg a circular letter) can 53
be programmed so thaat the system stops at designa- 104
ted points (stop codes) during print out. Then 155
either the operator manually keys in the specific 205
information (eg a name and address, and personal- 256
ised salutation) OR such information is inserted 307
automatically from a separately created list. The 359
latter is also known as LIST PROCESSING or MERG- 412 . . . . mins
ING. Thus a 'personalised' circular letter is 463
produced for each recipient. 492 . . . . Kdpm

A SYSTEM is a group of components - keyboard, 47 . . . . mins
screen, printer, etc - connected to function as a 97
unit, eg a word processor or computer. 136 . . . . Kdpm

A SYSTEMS ANALYST is a specialist who examines in 51
detail an existing method, and designs a system 99
which performs a similar job with the aid of a 146
computer. This requires knowledge of the busi- 195
ness side of the firm as well as of computers. 242
Systems analysts have to advise on hardware, 288
software, which programming language to use, as 336
well as designing forms for the input and output 385 . . . . mins
of information. 401 . . . . Kdpm

A WIDOW LINE is the first line of a paragraph 47
which appears by itself at the bottom of a page of 98
text. Widow lines spoil the appearance of printed 150
text, and systems can find them and readjust page 200 . . . . mins
lengths to get rid of them. See also ORPHAN LINE. 254 . . . . Kdpm

Kd

Word processors produce text that can be electro-   52

nically edited, printed, stored, and retrieved. Any   106

number of copies can be automatically run off, each one   162

of high-quality print. Word processors can also be   215

used in electronic mail systems for the instantaneous   269

transmission of text - over long distances if need be -   325

to other compatible systems.   354

The office uses to which a word processor can be   404

put are many and varied. Its versatility in correcting   461

and amending text makes it invaluable for the produc-   515

tion (without rekeying) of documents that usually need   572

some revision of the original draft - reports, surveys,   628

analyses, articles, etc. The machine automatically re-   685

formats pages after text-editing.   719

Information requiring periodic updating, such as   769

price lists and mailing lists, can be stored on disc   822

and then recalled, text-edited and printed out without   877

the need for retyping in full.   908

Word processors are especially useful for standard   960

correspondence and other standard documents. Standard   1016

letters, paragraphs, etc, are keyed in, checked, coded,   1072

and stored on disc, ready for high-speed automatic   1123

print out as required. The machine can be programmed   1178

to stop where variables need to be keyed in manually,   1232

or the merge facility is used for their automatic in-   1286

sertion from a separately created list. It is easy to   1342

see how word processors can save a great deal of time   1396

in the production of contracts and other legal docu-   1449

ments with standard clauses.   1478

. . . . mins

. . . . kdpm

. . . . mins

. . . . kdpm

. . . . mins

. . . . kdpm

Appendix B

Short drills to rectify weaknesses and build strengths.

A   as an at and are bad say said face state
      Alastair said that all was black at sea.

B   fbf be by bad bit able been boils bubble
      Babs obeyed but Mabel rebuked both boys.

C   dcd can act cut ice cash fact back cocoa
      Dick chose cake, and cut a choice slice.

D   day did dog dig had made laid done dated
      Send Ede down and don't do added damage.

E   ded let eat tea set ease seat time clear
      When we see the beech tree we are there.

F   if of far fly fir for fix life left fear
      Effy fears for her life if foxes follow.

G   fgf gap age ago beg gave gift page going
      Give Ginger's giggling girls a good hug.

H   jhj had his her has have help hope share
      Hugh Hope thought the Heath church high.

I   kik aim him lip pit live mine find faint
      Iris, write his initials inside the lid.

J   jag jar jug job jack ajar joke jump just
      Jo's joy in June is juicy jam and jelly.

K   key kid kit ask ink kick knot work stack
      Kay likes to take her book back quickly.

L   lay let lid lot old last leak lift level
      Lulled by low melodies, all fell asleep.

M   jmj map may met arm move harm same madam
      Tommy Mitchell mimed Miriam from memory.

N   jnj any not win can send seen none known
      In noon sunshine Nina nodded and snored.

O   lol oak ore oar off coal sold solo folio
      Bo took photos from our top-room window.

P   ;p; pay peg pig top open upon stop paper
      Piper propped up Pippa's apple saplings.

Q   aqa quay quite quiet quota squad quality
      Raquel quietly requested an equal quota.

R frf red rob bar art rare roar rear razor
Roberta reared three rare brown rabbits.

S as is us so say saw sit sum use sun sure
As soon as is safe, ask Susie to assist.

T ftf tap the put out part tape stop treat
Attract its attention with that trumpet.

U juj use our you buy unit full burn usual
You must surely guard such a full purse.

V fvf vast very over save give valve verve
Vivien Eve lives in clover in Avon Vale.

W sws was now who new what when were water
When we want water we walk to Swan Well.

X sxs axe tax box six exist excuse complex
Rex Baxter fixed up six extra wax boxes.

Y jyj any yes yet you year play rely early
Yes, try YESTERDAY for your yearly play.

Z aza size zinc zone zero maze azure blaze
No dazzling prize for zeal to lazy Suzy.

Right-hand shift Ada Sue Dan Fay Gus Wynn Eva Rob Ted Zoe
Brenda was X-rayed by Dr V C Quinn FRCS.

Left-hand shift Yul Una Ian Olly Pam Huw Jim Kay Lil May
Major Paul K Hill MP lives in Nash Mews.

Figures a1a s2s d3d f4f f5f j6j j7j k8k 191 ;00;
She paid on 24 May 86, cheque 0351 9678.

Alphabet/comma a, b, c, d, e, f, g, h, i, j, k, l, m,
n, o, p, q, r, s, t, u, v, w, x, y, z,

Alphabet/colon a: b: c: d: e: f: g: h: i: j: k: l: m:
n: o: p: q: r: s: t: u: v: w: x: y: z:

Alphabet/space bar a b c d e f g h i j k l m n o p q r s t
u v w x y z a b c d e f g h i j k l m n

Alphabet/shift keys a A b B c C d D e E f F g G h H i I j J
k K l L m M n N o O p P q Q r R s S t T
u U v V w W x X y Y z Z a A b B c C d D

Difficult reaches

ab/ba	able bad abut bar crab tuna stab ball baby rumba table debar
be/eb	be ebb bed web bear debt best ebony cube pebble better rebel
br/rb	brag barb brew garb sabre curb fibre arbour bribe verb brunt
bt/tb	debt outboard obtain setback subtle cutback obtrude outbreak
ce/ec	cede sect cedar elect fact echo accept direct space eclectic
cr/rc	cry arc crag arch acre perch craze farce secret mercy scrubs
ct/tc	act etch sect latch tact match tract pitch erect crutch fact
ev/ve	eve vet every very even ever never verve event serve devolve
in/ni	ink nib din nip pin nil pint nine mine unit link snib lining
ly/yl	fly style ply nylon sly pylon only idyll ally sylvan finally
mp/pm	amp topmost lamp upmost stamp deepmost amply chapman complex
mu/um	mud gum mug hum mule sum muse bump mute dump must lump mumps
my/ym	my hymn army nymph myth thyme myosis lymph myrrh rhyme mummy
no/on	not ton now won nod don snow bond know font knot onion north
ny/yn	any lynx nylon lynch tiny syntax nymph synod pony cynic puny
oy/yo	boy you coy yoyo ahoy your soya yoga decoy young alloy youth
py/yp	spy gypsy copy hypo pylon hypnosis happy crypts pygmy hyphen
rv/vr	derv oeuvre carve curve louvre nerve verve service manoeuvre

Bottom row

Nan became numb with excitement when the bomb was excavated.
Many convicts in C Annex heard Bob's name and number called.
I can economize by combining maximum use with minimum waste.

Home row

At last a sigh, a kiss and a keepsake sealed a sad farewell.
Sally sells jade, sea shells and glass flasks; Jake assists.
At all meals Stella has had alaska salad and a dash of salt.

Third row

With typewriter and a quire of paper we were quite equipped.
The queen of the upper river territory requires a new route.
Pepper, pottery and pewter ware were products of their work.

Appendix C

Royal Society of Arts Examinations Board — KEYBOARD SKILLS (Stage I)

Course requirements: The Board makes no requirement that candidates should have taken a course. (For the guidance of those who choose to, approximately 15 hours tuition is suggested as appropriate for this syllabus for a beginner.)

Form of test: A 10-minute copying test from material consisting of word, figure and alphanumeric strings; 'blocking' work (eg a 'computer entry' block); continuous text.

A hard copy of the keyed in work must be produced: if the test is carried out on screen-based equipment, production of the copy can be done by a tutor or supervisor.

Criteria of assessment: 99% accuracy at a minumum speed of 4,500 kdph (75 kdpm). The certificates of successful candidates will record the actual speed attained, rounded up or down to the nearest 5 key depressions.

Two past RSA KEYBOARD SKILLS examination papers follow on the next five pages. Follow the RSA instructions, which follow.

1 At the start of the text you will be instructed to insert a sheet of paper in your typewriter, or to create your own 'document', then to key in your name and the name of the centre.

  You will then be allowed 10 minutes to copy the material overleaf.

2 If you finish the material before the end of 10 minutes you may go back to the beginning and start again.

3 You must copy the text material exactly, using the same spacing and the same line endings.

4 Candidates using machines without a character 'Ø' may use either figure '0' or an upper case letter 'O'.

5 Candidates using machines without a figure '1' may use a lower case letter 'l' (el).

6 You may use techniques, *appropriate to your equipment*, to make corrections.

7 For award of a Pass you should complete at least the first half of the material and achieve 99% accuracy.

Rally Regulation Stage Reference Road
SCRUTINEER SERVICE MARSHAL SYMBOL

1123 45 33247 68 5543 5677 3322 2588410
00100111 0536 529 8741 5369101 5589063

Gp A (up to 1300cc) 1st VNsr/VAgte 84
Gp B (ov 2000cc) 1st Mrx7/VWGgti 83

```
RS No  Serv  Map
A      SA A  108
7B     SA 7  117
All    SA 1  79
```

A target time is given for each RS.
Competitors are allowed a maximum of
thirty minutes free of penalty between
rest halts. If this period is exceeded,
there is a penalty for each minute of
lateness up to a maximum of sixty
minutes. Any competitor exceeding
lateness in excess of sixty minutes will
be excluded. Early arrival is
permitted.

```
LET L1=L1+1
GOTO 145
IF E$=S$(N,N)
THEN 1690
copyd0 to d1
```

DELICATESSEN SWEETS TOBACCO BUILDING
Freehold Rateable Vendor Agent Acre

2444 2286 11545 2536 9968 247 92566601
8311811 157535 27 64211 9865 249347 501

Busy junc; Ples res; 1-up; S/S; lge/dg
kit, 3 beds; o-p; RV430: 50,000 sav MW/1

```
Type  Price  R/V
N/Ag  90500  1050
S/Pr  15950  387
O/L   46000  655
```

A very lucrative old established family
business selling only the best vehicles.
This valuable freehold site comprises
garage workshop, showroom area, petrol
pumps and a superb car pitch. There is
also a magnificent detached residence
offering panoramic views over lovely
countryside. This property is highly
recommended. Telephone to view.

```
DIM A(100)
PRINT "Valid"
header clt,ir
TIME (hh:mm(:ss))
```

Wth	Cat No	Pr
27"	93/wt	2.25
36"	93/TR	3.75
6'	78/wr	5.90

As children's feet grow rapidly, it is better to order one half or full size larger than the shoes being worn. When trying on new shoes there should be approximately one half of an inch between the tip of the longest toe and the end of the shoe. The toes should be able to spread freely and the foot should not be cramped at its widest point.

CATALOGUE OFFER SANDAL DENIM COTTON
Brown Sideboard Price Special Budget

62/SN 558 Ultra 23 P Pan @ 29.99 - 3 wks
dely cust - EX93a/dir line 061 876-3334

2124 358965 5 88967 5632 5699670012 112
1101 11 56 985336 74986 3256965 898 96

650 IF F=4 THEN GOTO 900
350 PRINT "answer is";$
chkdsk B:

Pcy no	Gross	Net
*3b/67	5.00	4.12
*8f/9j	29.75	27.63
*3a/31	nil	

The endowment plan of the society combines the best features of many of the existing contracts by providing the maximum of investment flexibility after ten years with the facility to extend some of the options for a further ten years. In order to achieve this degree of flexibility you must initially agree to pay contributions for twenty years.

ASSURANCE BENEFITS INCOME CAPITAL LIFE
Medically Insurance Premiums Value

CBS PNo. DCR5270 (Ag 2.7.25) Ren Dt 8
Nov 85 poly hodr Jones B - Prem 41.60

5242 36 9856 32015 202 202 63 65995 561
1998 65893 256 9822 558255 54885637 74

10 OPEN "O",1,"LIST"
110 A$=SPACE$(20)
1205 RSET A$=N$

Appendix D

Pitman Examinations Institute —
KEYBOARDING (Intermediate)

Course requirements: Candidates should have an accurate copying speed for alphanumeric data of at least 17 wam (5,100 key depressions per hour) before attempting this examination.

Form of test: The examination will consist of 4 questions, timed separately. Any form of erasing is allowed. Candidates will be required to:

1 Check incorrect copy against correct copy and to circle a given number of errors in 3 minutes.

2 Type for 7 minutes material consisting of 700 strokes (using the standard word count) with the emphasis on the alphabet keys. (There will be a 2-minute break at the end of this question.)

3 Type for 10 minutes material consisting of 800 strokes, with the emphasis on the signs and symbols.

4 Type for 10 minutes material consisting of 800 strokes, with the emphasis on the numbers.

Criteria of assessment: In the proofreading question and question **2**, two errors only are permitted and candidates must achieve a 98% accuracy (no more than 3 errors in each) in questions **3** and **4** to gain a Pass.

The following errors will carry a penalty of 1:

- each letter, number or character missing, additional, unrecognisable, wrong, piled, clearly above or below the writing line
- each space (or spaces in one location) omitted or in excess
- each transposition: letters, numbers, words or characters
- each incorrect line spacing
- each margin irregularity which is clearly not attributable to mechanical defect

The following errors will carry a penalty of 2:

- overtyping
- each word omitted or in excess

The following error will carry a penalty of 3:

- omission or addition of a whole line

A past PEI KEYBOARDING examination paper follows on the next four pages.

1 Read through the copy below, checking it against the correct copy
 in Question 3. There are 15 errors or omissions in this piece.
 Mark the errors with a circle where they occur.

 You have 3 minutes to do this.

The 'Panavision" video which we at DAY & SON have been

offering at a very high discount for 3 weeks was an

extremely popular model and we had no problems selling our

enormous stocks(even though we had been very optimitic) .

The featurss which appealled most seemed to be the 14-day

4 programmable timer, the cue/review operation and the

infrared remote control. The light-emiting diodes are

clearly visible from 10' and the unit fits neatly under most

televisoin sets. It is a "good looking" unit which should

not look out of place in the average lounge room.It is

possible to record for as long as 4 hours on the REN-240

casette tape and of course the built-in timer offers

a Lot of flexibility!

2 *Type the following, beginning a new line where indicated.*

You have 10 minutes to do this question.

These generous discounts were allowed: (new line)
10% to £99; 15% to £499; 17.5% to £999 & 25% to £1500.   (new line)

The metal rod was available in 2 different sizes: (new line)
9" x 1" (228.6 mm x 25.4 mm) & 10" x 2" (254 mm x 50.8 mm).   (new line)
(Aluminium available in sizes 9" x 1" & 2".)   (new line)

Make a note of these important details: (new line)
(1) name*; (2) age; (3) occupation; (4) address*.   (new line)
*Please put these 2 details first.   (new line)

Answer "Yes" or "No" to these questions: (new line)
a) "Is it raining?"   (new line)
b) "Is today's date the 24th?"   (new line)
c) "Will you be travelling abroad next month?"   (new line)

Please write these equations carefully: (new line)
Y = X + 13, A = B - (C + D) x (C - (D + 2) x 3).   (new line)

The invoice was made up as follows: (new line)
XX/43 16 tables @ £210.50 (£3368.00) - 10% = £3031.20   (new line)
XY/78 64 chairs @ £75.95 (£4860.80) - 12.5% = £4253.20   (new line)
YX/65 12 settees @ £550.00 (£6600.00) - 5% = £6270.00

Type the following, beginning a new line where indicated.

You have 7 minutes to do this question.

The "Panavision" video which we at DAY & SONS have been   (new line)
offering at a <u>very</u> high discount for 3 weeks was an   (new line)
extremely popular model and we had no problems selling our   (new line)
enormous stocks (even though we had been very optimistic).   (new line)
The features which appealed most seemed to be the 14 day   (new line)
4 programmable timer, the cue/review operation and the   (new line)
infrared remote control. The light-emitting diodes are   (new line)
clearly visible from 10' and the unit fits neatly under most   (new line)
television sets. It is a "good-looking" unit which should   (new line)
not look out of place in the average lounge room. It is   (new line)
possible to record for as long as 4 hours on the RE-N240   (new line)
cassette tape and of course the built-in timer offers   (new line)
a <u>LOT</u> of flexibility!

4 Type the following, beginning a new line where indicated.

You have 10 minutes to do this question.

French classes will be offered at these times: (new line)
Monday 14 July: 0930 - 1030, Room 147 or 149 (new line)
Tuesday 15 July: 1000 - 1100, Room 28 or 30 (new line)

Periods of time are indicated as follows: (new line)
4 hours 10 minutes, 3 hours 8 minutes. (new line)

All books must have an International Standard Book Number: (new line)
0 273 01477 0, 0 273 46113 4, 0 273 97900 3, 0 273 33901 1. (new line)

National Insurance numbers should be carefully recorded: (new line)
2T 634143A, 2X 499862B, 2R 779831C, 3T 865540B. (new line)
4T 200044C, 7Y 103479M, 8B 602337A, 9T 634800C. (new line)

Study these speed limits and note the nearest kilometre: (new line)
45 mph - nearest is 70 km/h - 43.7 miles/hour. (new line)
60 mph - nearest is 100 km/h - 62.5 miles/hour. (new line)

The auction includes: (new line)
Lot 1 - 320,472 acres; Lot 2 - 147,002 acres; (new line)
Lot 3 - 210,620 acres; Lot 4 - 104,755 acres; (new line)
Lot 5 - 414,788 acres; Lot 6 - 113,399 acres.

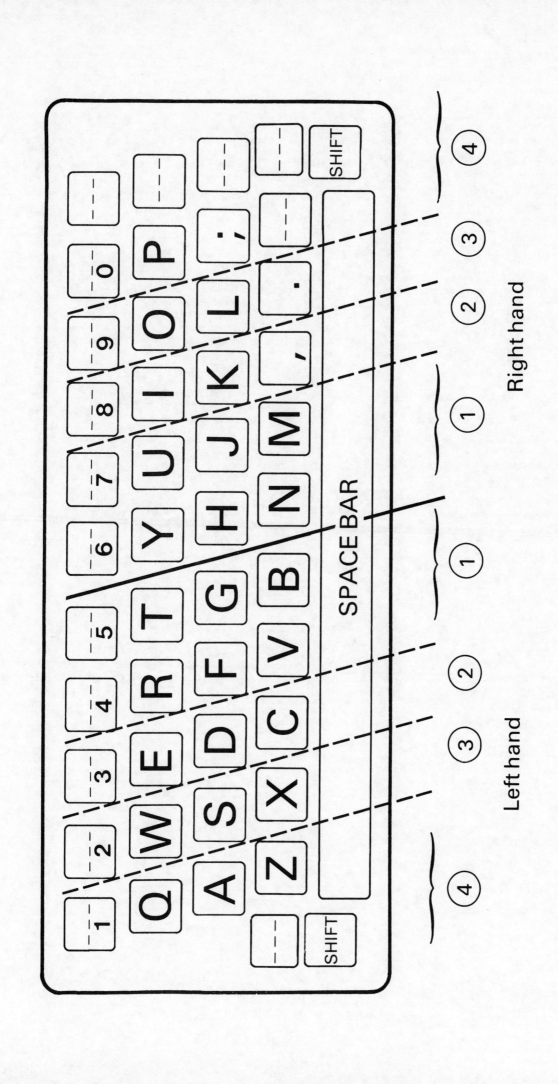